# *Mouth*

Also by James Sutherland-Smith

Books and Pamphlets

*Four Poetry and Audience Poets* P&A, Leeds 1971
*A Poetry Quintet* Gollancz, London 1976
*The Death of Orpheus* Words Etc., London 1976
*Trapped Water* Earthgrip, London 1977
*Death of a Vixen* Many Press, London 1978
*A Singer from Sabiya* Many Press, London 1979
*Naming of the Arrow* Salamander Imprint, London 1981
*The Country of Rumour* Many Press, London 1985
*At the Skin Resort* Arc Publications, Todmorden 1999
*In the Country of Birds* Carcanet, Manchester 2003
*Popeye in Belgrade* Carcanet, Manchester 2008

Translations *(with Viera Sutherland-Smith except where stated)*

*Not Waiting for Miracles* Modrý Peter, Levoca 1993
(with Štefánia Allen and V S-S)
*Slovensky balady* Pavian Records, Bratislava 1995
(with Zuzanna Homolová)
*Swallowing a Hair. Poems by Ján Ondruš,* Studna, Bratislava 1998
(with Martin Solotruk)
*An Album of Slovak Writers,* Bratislava 2000
*100 Years of Slovak Literature,* Bratislava / Vilenica, Slovenia 2000
*Cranberries in Ice: Selected Poems of Ivan Laučík*
Modrý Peter, Canada 2001
*The Melancholy Hunter: Selected Poems of Ján Buzassy*
Modrý Peter, Canada 2001
*Scent of the Unseen. Selected Poems of Mila Haugová*
Arc Publications, Todmorden 2002
*And That's the Truth: Selected Poems of Milan Rúfus*
Bolchazy-Carducci Publishers, Mundelein, IL. 2005
*Dinner with Fish and Mirrors: Selected Poems of Ivana Milankov*
Arc Publications, Todmorden, 2013
*Selected Poems of Miodrag Pavlovic,* Salt Publications, Cromer, 2014

James Sutherland-Smith

# *Mouth*

Shearsman Books

First published in the United Kingdom in 2014 by
Shearsman Books
50 Westons Hill Drive
Emersons Green
BRISTOL
BS16 7DF

Shearsman Books Ltd Registered Office
30–31 St. James Place, Mangotsfield, Bristol BS16 9JB
(this address not for correspondence)

www.shearsman.com

ISBN 978-1-84861-353-9



Acknowledgements
Some of these poems have appeared on-line in these ezines and blogs: *The Bow-Wow Shop, Ink, Sweat and Tears, Peony Moon, Qualm* and Norm Sibum's blog.

# Introduction

Randall Jarrell, since his death a poet of fluctuating reputation, but to me a master of line and the expression of feeling, prefaced his *Selected Poems* with an introduction as opposed to the orthodox practice of appending notes at the end of the collection. He justified this by writing that when giving readings he always said something about a poem before he read it and that in Wordsworth's and Tennyson's collected poems there were "hundreds of pages of notes and prefaces and reminiscences." It seems eminently sensible to me to write something by way of an introduction especially as it is a poem that draws on a variety of sources. The difficulty is, of course, to write enough to intrigue readers, but not so much that their readings are channelled into a narrow, author-made ditch of response. A second difficulty is to avoid making the poem sound so daunting that the reader replaces it back on the shelf in a bookshop with the feeling of having had a narrow escape. With these pitfalls in mind I've tried to indicate themes, motifs and sources in a coherent fashion. More detailed acknowledgment is given at the end of the poem.

The poem's central image is the human mouth and its relationship to human utterances whether in speech or song and poetry. It begins at my cabin in Eastern Slovakia drawing on nature and human love. By section 26 the poem sets off on its travels by way of Egypt, Arabia, Persia, Afghanistan into Classical China where there is a slight failure to communicate. In 43 Sophia withdraws from direct communication. Back at the cabin the poem worries over a mouth's relation to poetry and gets itself into such a fix that by 51 there is an attempt to communicate with a stone. The stone's reply in 52 is very simple and the moon's in 53 is even simpler.

The second part of the poem attempts to identify the absent Sophia and then moves away to a number of unsatisfactory mouthings; religion, dysfunctional relationships, politics, diplomacy, the military and commerce. After confessing to a failure of nerve it travels to Venice by way of Budapest before returning to rest among a monastic community, a possible reunion with Sophia and then towards last things. The old poet in the last section is Ezra Pound.

My daughter, Katarina, appears early in the poem and then again towards the end. At the beginning she is succeeded by my wife, Viera. A coincidence in my life is that my first love was called Vera. She and my wife signify the beginning and culmination of my passionate affections. In 21 Viera changes into Sophia, the divine woman of the Gnostics. For the Orthodox Church Sophia is the personification of divine wisdom, but in Gnosticism she is a multiple personality, the mother of the divinity that some call Jehovah and a 'fallen' woman in both spiritual and social senses of the word. She retains her attributes of wisdom, but it is wisdom equivalent to the experience of Blake's songs. When the sequence moves into Asia she becomes identified with the Chinese goddess, the Queen of the West, who offered immortality to a number of Chinese emperors who subsequently failed to attain it.

A recurring motif in the poem is that of the bee and "bee-stung lips". The bee has a world-wide divine significance. Orphic teaching compares bees swarming from the hive to souls swarming from the divine unity. In Ancient Greece and Rome Sophocles and Virgil were supposed to have had their lips touched by honey in extreme infancy and in India and China eloquence was a gift conferred by honey. The Semitic root "dbr" is cognate with "word' and "honey". Bee-stung lips are not only an alluring feature of silent movie stars, but an attribute of Sophia in the poem and poets whose words wound them. The image has been with me ever since the second poem I wrote worth publishing at the age of twenty, which had the phrase "with bees still buzzing in my words."

The poem also includes ants, beetles, a toad or two, birds and flowers. Flowers are images for the mouth as are insects in a more indirect way. Insects don't use their mouthparts for communication, but for the most for eating. Ants communicate with their sense of smell and their antennae and bees have their dance. Birds use song, but not for artistic purposes, instead for attracting a mate, warning, and asserting territorial rights. I am also attracted by the notion that human speech may have begun as song and by recent research into whether we have any element of Neanderthal man in our DNA. There's a wonderful novel by William Golding, *The Inheritors*, which imagines their passing in the face of competition from Homo sapiens sapiens.

A number of writers are tutelary presences in the poem. The phrase "What's that buzzing?" comes from Samuel Beckett's, *Not I,* whose first performance by Billie Whitelaw is the origin of section 64. Geoffrey Hill's trilogy of long poems published at the turn of the millennium impelled me to write eight of the sections in *Mouth* although these have been transformed as my initial reaction of bafflement has been replaced by wonder at his prescience at events in the conduct of British politics over the last ten years. Gottfried Benn provided me with some morbid imagery in 24 and 30. His "internal exile" in Germany during the Nazi years is a strategy, which troubles me. In 80 Viera and I counsel each other to cowardice when confronted with decisions whether to intervene or refrain from direct action.

Rimbaud's sonnet, 'Voyelles,' on the vowels is a counter-balance to the four tones used in Chinese classical poetry. Three of the sequence, 40, 41 and 42, contain poems composed from material in three poems by Ts'en Shen (715-770) a poet of the Tang dynasty who was stationed in the west of China. I have imagined him near the Tien Shan range. I have followed a poem by Jules Laforgue more closely in 50 as a light-headed way of getting the sequence out of the metaphysical fix that it was drifting towards almost halfway through.

The supreme image of a mouth in medieval literature, possibly unsurpassable in any literature, is the unveiling of Beatrice's mouth in Canto 31 in *Purgatorio*. This comes in for some profane treatment in 57 and 58.

Ezra Pound is an active ghost in the poem and manifests himself in 83 as a young man, a drone bee in 85 and then as an old poet climbing Tien Shan in the last section. The range of reference in the poem owes its arbitrary diversity to his example in *The Cantos* although I hope its temper is less offensive, if its theme is considerably narrower.

Brief appearances are made by John Ruskin, Sandro Botticelli, Francis Bacon the painter, and Giovanni Gabrieli (1553-1612) the measure of whose grave yet radiant music I've sought to reflect in the poem. The practice of *Cori spezzati*, dividing musical forces over space to contrast, echo, and respond and, from time to time, to unite harmoniously informed the deployment of motifs in the poem.

The penultimate section is addressed to the late Edwin Morgan (1920–2010). The poem was written in 2008, but he died as I was putting the poem into its final order.

1.

A gap in the trees,
water accelerating through
two lumpy boulders
that narrow the brook,
the cabin door ajar:

swallows can nip through trees
taking midges on the wing,
a toad can hop
on to a rough surface
from the cool element

it swims in easily,
I can appear, hair spiky,
for my early morning piss,
all of us a word forming
the moment a mouth opens.

2.

Water drop round as the letter O,
a single contraction of my mouth,
therefore pure as a vowel can get
until gravity tugs a leaf to let
water run and me to eavesdrop

on conversation upon stone, tin and earth
whose meaning is hard to make out
though possibly I'm not meant to
as from darkness into a world unshaped,
loose, liquid that absorbs my footsteps,

I move, rubbing the sleep from my eyes
so as my vision clears discourse blurs.
The robin's throat quivers and gives forth
neither recognition nor a threat.
In the stream mineral on mineral scrapes.

3.

Or to go at the beginning of spring
when sound is not ghostly but mineral.
The creak in the brook is ice breaking.
Then I blink as the light slides down twigs
like an eagerness to do something novel;

a melting, my daughter has pointed out,
hanging on the tips of pine needles;
to describe the moment before their weight
causes them to fall as innocence
or ignorance is not simple.

I am blinded and cannot see
through a scattering of old snow crystals.
Is this rebirth or an opportunity
to repeat error? I can't measure
the moment when each drop of water tumbles.

4.

Only a mouth can tremble
shapelessness into a perfect circle.
Geometry, a gun's hard muzzle
are absolutes bringing forth
pure silences of co-ordinates and death.

We should prefer forms which are impure;
eyes, almond-shaped, marred with lids and tears,
nostrils like kidney beans, inefficient ears,
complexity within complexity
into which truth passes and becomes perplexity.

Below our meanings the navel is a knot
of withered origin, below that
division between an early chordate
erect ever since the palaeozoic seas
and a vertical primness which can piss or please.

5.

A mouth is like a flowerhead
in long section. I imagine
bees clustered on the lips to feed
on the nectar issued by the tongue
or lips pursed for a humming bird

whose version of a kiss dartles
past lips, teeth to the throat
of a flower from where gutturals
of sweetness are sounded outwards
becoming angels' trumpet calls

for their creation of Adam
according to the Secret Book of John,
the lips by Banen-Ephroum,
teeth by Amen, molars Ibikan,
tonsils by Basiliademe.

6.

The yellow trumpet flower
declares nothing except
that the lovely and mundane
return in equal measure.
Ugliness and evil are required for understanding.

A mouth sounding a high A,
lips trembling round the note
like the sun's edges giving off flames,
that heat passing outwards through us.
Silence and the cold shape understanding.

And the vertical smile gapes
so that a head appears from it
covered in blood and muck,
red as though from rage.
Birth and death overwhelm understanding.

7.

As we travel back and back
to the beginning of our very own time
there's always a black hole
out of which our stars emerge
or simply our mother's birth canal

a passage at the end of which
is a blinding light, thus our birth
our first near-death experience
causing our eyes to be shut tight
as we hear sound other than mother's heart beat.

Is this why us old folk, brought up not to swear,
are still troubled by religion,
the first words we hear, "Oh my God! Jesus!"
Not our children hearing our wives' godly wit,
"Oh fuck, oh fuck, it hurts like shit!"

8.

Pushed out from another    a mouth opens wide
In a welter of blood    wailing in pain
And complaining greatly    completes great joy
Girning toothless lacking sense    it gives love sense
Utterance stopped with milk    praise songs horns of mead

Mouth opening on mouth    murmurs promise meaning
For two whole lives long    for two legs to open wide
Sighing sobbing greatly    suffer lovers to great joy
Gasping at conclusion    grinning like conquistadors
Utterance wonderstruck    at new world upon new world

Heeded with little patience    a mouth repeats its tale
Desire dwindling to memory    meaning melting away
Into witless confusion    whimpering like a child
Girning toothless lacking sense    lovelessly ignored
Utterance rattling to silence    to rictus a hole in stone

9.

Mouth a sepulchre
stone uprights topped
by stone lintel
or doorway more compactly
constructed in brick

or vagina toothless mouth
whether maid woman crone
I rose from the tomb
emerged covered in blood
initiated as more than beast

less than a god
my own mouth frames
matters of knowledge and,
to preserve mystery,
matters of evasion

10.

door:
*vacuum  hiatus  lacuna  space  gap*
*aperture  crack  slot  fissure  cavity*
*opening  hole  orifice  mouth  north and south*
*chops  kisser  trap  mush  gob*

threshold, lintel, jamb, handle, lock:
*lips  teeth  tongue  hard palate  tonsils*
*nose  nostrils  septum  sinus  soft palate*
*throat  pharynx  voice box  larynx  vocal fold*
*diaphragm  belly  lungs  what else?  breath*

swings to and fro on its hinges:
*breathe  exhale  sigh  moan  grunt  whistle*
*snarl  hiss  click  whoop  titter  snigger*
*guffaw  crow  giggle  wail  sob  bawl*
*bellow  trill  croon  hum  mumble  speak*

11.

Robin, great tit, blackcap, redstart,
thrush, fieldfare, wren and starling,
a woodpecker drumming on the bark
of the tall pines for beetles
and martins at full pelt squealing.

A slowworm flickers out of sight
between wild garlic and ragwort
under a briar rose's thorns
close to a grey wagtail chick so young
it can only flutter to a stone

in the middle of the brook
where it calls and calls while I look
at the orange throat of its desire,
the sign for a parent zipping
to the stone then dipping, dipping.

12.

Ragwort almost unnoticed
on our cabin's shadow side
under the maple's winged seed
idling down in soughs of air;
ragwort, multi-petalled, yellow,

a minor g-type star
barely visible to the eye,
inedible to all except
the cinnabar moth which thus
makes itself obnoxious to birds.

Is it one of the numberless
crowding my writing lamp at night
which are not to my taste either?
What consumes the cinnabar moth?
What devours otherness?

13.

As we travel back and back and back
beyond the beginning of our species' time,
beyond layers of ancestral memory,
each grave stratum, oak coffin, stone sarcophagus,
scraped hole, foetal crouch head pointing south,

we meet our most distant relatives,
Neanderthals, their huge nostrils
devised to warm cold air off the glaciers,
two black holes forested with nose hair
to filter wind-blown grit of loess and ice.

What was their language? Pitched between grunt and song?
Perhaps homo sapiens sapiens
borrowed an ability to croon
to babes in arms or lament or, so it seems,
to lay flowers on the bodies of the dead.

14.

For six years a wild rose has slowly grown.
A bare green loop of thorn
curves in winter over the frozen brook.
Snow does not cling to it,
a resistance easy enough to overlook.

In spring it snags my daughter's hair
when she stoops to wash smuts from the fire
her face pricked by cold to the pink
of the five petals that will bloom
and shed before we have time to think

of roses, which are impossible;
the rose, which is invisible
and unscented or its opposite,
the rose whose odour lingers in the grave,
whose black petals are infinite.

15.

Rose of truth (romantic notion!)
Rose of the tongue (surreal notation!)
Both can be dead-headed
by my secateurs, a sharp edge,
any working butcher's knife.

I think that truths are like the roses
climbing on my south-facing wall last June.
Their profusion might have been the consequence
of the wreaths of smoke I made last April
to protect buds on my apricots.

Though I saw roses like mine
everywhere in other gardens.
Think of their redness on others' lips,
a language of roses for a season.
Accuse me of allegory if you like.

16.

Rose chafer, green knight in miniature,
cumbersome in upper body armour
whose chitin can shimmer gold
at a slight angle to the sun,
underparts a jointed pure copper,

shinning the stalk of a white flower
in stops and starts like an elderly beachcomber
after coconuts, tiny head swivelling
as it munches pollen, legs notched for purchase,
it does not crawl, but clings to my knuckles

when I place on the edge of a petal
of a pink Jubilee rose
where it hangs like a jewel
from a pierced lip until it whirrs
helicopter rotor blades of wings and soars.

17.

Slow, dumb, wordless music of the mouth,
that pursing, twisting, indrawing of the lips
I know so well from a life
watching your face before I speak.
What can I say, white rose,

knowing that you've guessed already
what I'm about to ask or claim
or even observe on matters
important or trivial?
We smile at our smiles

so well do we respond to tiny muscles'
twitch, flicker and relax
that speech seems unrequired,
a ghostly exercise of breath
long after meaning taken.

18.

The word proceeding
from the darkness of the mouth,
from that moist warmth,
blood heat under the tongue,
knowledge becoming itself,

becoming itself in the act of speech,
brief stars born from a black hole,
a breath across the galaxy,
your tongue proceeding
from between your lips,

from between your lips
after stars have burnt themselves out,
your tongue tip stroking my lips.
touching the tip of my tongue,
a first kiss changing the universe.

19.

What does the universe taste like?
Almost like fresh milk
when the universe was twelve,
half Italian with thick hair
curling down to her waist,

Vera her name, a first love,
almost the same as my last,
Viera, meaning faith.
What does the universe taste of?
It tastes of faith

though other universes
came between first and last faith,
one returning something of myself,
my breath cached beneath her tongue,
a taste salty not unpleasant.

20.

Mouth becomes month
shrinks to moth
flaps across the moon
monstrous the shadow cast
mounts higher descends

towards man-made light
over my cabin's deck
where a month ago
your mouth closed on my mouth
quite without warning

our mouths, lips, tongues
becoming unbecoming
in their anarchy
your face in my hands
your lips severe with desire

21.

You drew yourself up over the edge
of the rock and stood hands akimbo
as sea water trickled from throat to thigh.
Some distance out a patrol boat passed
searching for contraband dropped at night.

Almost lazily you knelt, extended
your arms to me so I could pull you
down to become a word to be pronounced
over and over, mouths and tongues
becoming instruments of touch not sense.

"I wish to give birth to God," you said,
douching yourself with the clear brine above
sea anemones and urchins fringed
with orange tentacles or purple spikes
around mouths that swallow and excrete.

22.

I watch your mouth go through its motions,
not an O but tall as a zero,
nothingness framed by flesh which relaxes,
lightly compresses to bee-stung composure,
pouts in amusement, almost the motions

of a word though only a sigh escapes,
whether from boredom or satisfaction
I can’t tell for certain stooping
to catch exactly what it is you say
as you turn your head and your mouth escapes

to breathe on to the dressing table mirror
as you apply a little lipstick
and will not let me kiss you.
We have dressed, the sea some way off
beyond the window, not a mirror.

23.

A mouth with lips of a different texture
from the leaves surrounding them
sniggers in the laurel, which stirs
just before a slow rustle
like a blackbird hopping over leaf mould.

I make my way cautiously
round the shrub not wishing
to frighten anyone or anything.
A few white polystyrene cups
flecked with drops of red wine gape at me.

In the secret wood of what I wished to say
the leaves are pieces of torn manuscript
desiccated and foxed with age.
I've missed the party and the girl who might have
given me a kiss to put flesh on my bones.

24.

A mouth shapes itself
when it holds a note in song
so that sounds may come
without interruption
from belly and throat.

Sometimes lips quiver
from the force of sound, not feeling.
So, pursed or wide open,
a mouth strains towards roundness,
towards perfection.

Not on the mind of Gottfried Benn
stooping over a corpse:
*The mouth of a girl*
*who had lain long in the reeds*
*looked so chewed up.*

25.

At the end of the valley,
beeches on the crest of the hill,
behind them, late at night,
the waning moon unveiling itself
as a lopsided smile,

over a campfire whispering light
from which a girl, a wraith,
drifts to me. Where is my art?
With faith, tucked up at home in bed
as the girl warms herself at my hearth.

"As long as you like," I mutter.
Her full lips pout as if to say
something as the boy lurches in
guilt-stricken or jilted,
gawping at her, in the way.

26.

Language beginning as song,
a meld of whistles, grunts, sighs,
feeling trying to be precise
about number, distance, time.
Forget it! Young mouths open,

cigarette lighters flicked on
over their heads and chanting
as they wave until their thumbs burn
and the poem forms its complex word
for my mouth to pronounce;

language forcing meaning into song
and failing much too often.
All my life I have worried
about number, distance, time
and now they worry at me.

27.

There are higher voices than ours
whose lower harmonics
don't chime with our natural pitch,
Not even with a semi- or micro-tone's dissonance.
They're like a sore or an itch;

angels or demons or tinnitus
due to age and decay of the soul.
Demons, I think, for angels bless
and I can still enter silence;
the proof of sound is its absence.

Demons whisper, if it can be called that,
like noise from a crossed line
which is always a peevish whine
of someone complaining; in a dream last night
they hissed, "Oo muss lemme essplain."

28.

*but I was pursued*
*by the very vivid impression*
*that wet lips were whispering into my ear*
*with great rapidity and emphasis*
*for some time together*

In the morning I saw its mouth
squirming over the grass
and then, like a thick red elastic band flicked,
suddenly it wasn't there
leaving a track of nothingness,

which the grass healed with a lush growth.
Though ever after I've sensed a hidden line
where it was, without any width whatever,
just infinite depth beneath the roots
over which I step with infinite care.

29.

Almost forgotten voices sift up
like the vapours of the morning dew
from the invisible rift in the grass
that runs through one neighbour's garden
all round the world back through the other neighbour's fence.

"You looking up my skirt, you naughty boy?"
A misty image of a lipsticked mouth,
pouting from the top of a builder's ladder,
screened on the back of the Sheikh's palace
overlooking a Red Sea port.

I, as ever, fearing a trap,
therefore opt for the decorous,
"I preferred the Bruce Lee movie,"
shortly before the night time call to prayer.
"You no like girls?" "Oh yes, but veiled."

30.

Being or not-being in this life;
now you see it now you don't;
now you hear its song, now you don't;
now you smell, now your eyes sting
like my brother's in Kuwait from a whiff

of the action in Basra. Is it enough
just to stay put in the life you've chosen?
I confess I'm not one of the chosen
few who affect the otherness
around them. I'd like to stay aloof,

like Gottfried Benn amputate the brain's strife,
So roses blooming through the skull and mouth.
*I had to reach through the chest*
*under the skin to cut out the tongue*
*and palate with a long knife.*

31.

The Persian dentist with the florid English
beckoned to his dainty nurse to come
and marvel at a splendid example
of what he said was a very well-kept mouth,
a pleasing interior, he continued,

in stark contrast to the jagged peaks
and defiles it was his melancholy lot
to remove, replace and manicure.
I smiled as best I could, though that's not easy
when one's mouth is held open by metal clamps.

With his thumb tips he pressed a white gold crown
on the peg he'd made of what remained
of my left lower molar tooth.
It's still there. Superb work, other dentists say
when they hear the story of its origins.

32.

In the desert the sound of those who speak
is either a childish treble or an ancient croak.
Sometimes the wind whimpers round a rock
then fizzles through sand, gravel and stone
like the speech of something unborn.

Sometimes on any of the old Silk roads
you hear wings rattle like the slats
in the jalousies of the home you quit
as the rock doves chuckle above your head
gliding to pools left by a flash flood.

When you go with your empty canteen
you find tracks where the unknown has been
to drink its fill. Is this what hisses,
grunts, chortles through the night? You lie sleepless
until morning when you thank God, lift up your voice.

33.

Echo, ricochet, deja vu;
what you say comes back to you
reminding that you're guilty, too.
What is a poor boy to do
when you're trapped with no way through?

Words forgotten beyond recall
are like ignorance before the Fall.
The words return and appal
with errors you hoped forestalled.
That's what happens when you promise all.

You turn your compass on your chart.
A dislodged pebble makes you start.
Faster than sound, aimed at your heart
is what you fear denies your art;
the No which will tear you apart.

34.

What's that buzzing, becoming an angry drone,
becoming a pulsing of rotor blades
as an olive green helicopter flips over
the jagged edges of a saddleback pass,
with its gun turrets swivelling like insect mouthparts

close to where the Akoond of Swat
was once prodded into a limerick
by the Celtic regiments, now long gone
over the hills and far away from the grikes
and clints hiding passionate bearded snipers,

though their snapshots, their executions of those
who stray from submission grow more sporadic
the further we progress to Western China,
that Central Asia of remote origin,
where they practised pure conversation?

35.

Not that poetry is conversation,
a one-way trafficking directed at
anyone fool enough to listen,
the pure lyric cry, used air at blood heat
tripped and diverted over the palate.

And as for pure conversation;
it emerges from dark red learning
where desire for nothing is foolish yearning,
an abyss of inanition
below the tulip's daily opening and closing.

Desire replaces understanding with an itch.
You'll be deafened by the four tones.
Listen to the mountain's perfect pitch,
the sound of water rustling down
from the high passes over stones.

36.

The character for mouth, k’ou,

口

a vertical stroke on the left, a horizontal for the base,
the third touch a right angle looped over,
three strokes to make four sides,
three into four that goes.

All the passes across the roof of the world
have mouth as suffix as have some river towns.
Do they inhale the traveller in summer,
blow him out with snow in winter?
I seek the Queen of the West, her gift of immortality.

Let’s return to the character, more door than mouth.
Stand in front of the mirror (Go on! Don’t be shy!)
and pull faces and you’ll see your mouth is curved
like space and can speak infinite sentences
going on and on as I think you think I will.

37.

Forgive me my poor ear,
but I prefer the sound of Rameau
to that of Rimbaud,
arrangement to derangement,
acoustic principle to synaesthesia.

I have tiptoed round the borders
or arrived too early or too late
at the scenes of great disorders.
Better to gaze at sleeping eyelids
than the wide stare of the dead.

Rameau was once played for the Emperor of China.
The Jesuits could imagine nothing finer.
The Son of Heaven turned up his nose.
Cultural difference, I suppose,
not a lack of taste by the Emperor of China.

38.

Arthur may well have been right,
a future of cheap comix and Readers' Wives
though nothing in his work would lead us to dream
of a snuff movie's artistic unity;
orgasm and real terror in a single scream.

Language's saving grace is not the Word,
simply that it's only language.
The Marquis de Sade is horrid,
but still better than blows to the head,
which decades later cause Parkinson's Disease.

Language's damnation is the Word,
the symbol which transubstantiates a nothing
all too often into something to kill for.
I prefer to believe that my last gasp
could mean absolutely anything.

39.

Pure conversation will never come my way.
Dark red learning I already have
in the blood returning to my heart.
My lips are not bee-stung for the four tones.
Nor will I bind my hair in a top knot.

Arthur's five vowels can make me a shaman
from the time when speech was music:
A, the black bee, E, my white rose, I, the red,
U, the green rose chafer, O, the blue speedwell.
Though all is the desire the Gnostics shed

croaking name after name in breath foul with thirst
in the mountains behind Port Said
where I was conceived. Am I a parched sign?
The masters of the four tones lower their gaze,
their lips bee-stung and swollen from wine.

40. *(after a poem by Ts'en Shen)*

On Wheel Tower's walls the night bugle calls.
The buglers hawk spit from mouths dry as chalk
and the flags dangle at the northern angle
of the parapet where the look-out's set
to watch where a gust blows all to dust.

As the sun rises the Grand Army rouses
with bugles at dawn, drums loud as a storm.
The mountain vibrates from ten thousand shouts
and then not a sound at a word of command.
Just hear a pin drop as our general mounts up.

Shod hooves and shod feet will tramp through the sleet
over fields where the grass will hold the dead in its clasp.
At Blade River, fog. The wind howls like a dog.
At Sand Mouth sharp rocks, so old horseshoes break.
We endure each pain without thought of gain.

41. *(after a poem by Ts'en Shen)*

Look how far the river rolls to the snowy sea,
how sand from the desert twists up to the heavens
and shattered rocks undermined by the gale
slide so fast into the valleys we ride through,
our words of command muffled against cold and dust.

West of the gold hill smoke and ash roll in columns.
The whole night we must stand to in full armour
while the bitter wind squeezes our eyes and mouths to slits
and sweat steams then turns to frost on our horses' backs
leaving a five-petalled pattern under the saddle.

We'll be advanced with a clatter of weaponry.
Our general's challenge from an inkwell of ice
has snow-bitten the barbarian chieftain's heart.
We won't need to loose an arrow or cross swords.
We wait for news of his submission at the Western Pass.

42. *(after a poem by Ts'en Shen)*

The north wind whistles from its many mouths
and bends the white grass to breaking point.
The eighth month snow whirls like a spring gale's
flurry of pear blossom from a thousand trees.
It penetrates the blinds, wets the silk curtains.

His bee-stung mouth pouts from above a fur wrap.
The linen mat is too flimsy to warm his feet.
Our bows are rigid, can hardly be drawn.
Armour freezes, an unwanted second skin.
The sand sea dazzles and deepens with ice.

We drink to our guest now homeward bound.
At sunrise when snow drifts hug our tents
we watch him dawdle through Wheel Tower gate
going east into the mouth of the pass
until he vanishes leaving only hoof prints.

43.

Sophia wrote to me from Bishkek
with Tien Shan just to the east.
"I can tell you such stories
about the Celestial Mountain.
Once I almost walked on a cloud."

Now Sophia's decided to keep her feet
firmly planted on the ground
just because we might never meet.
I wonder what was gained in translation
when my letter was understood.

I look at the photo she sent.
A hint of pallor in her cheeks.
She'll walk alone with mist across the track
so that she seems to float between the peaks.
Outside my cabin dew glints like broken glass.

44.

Before dawn so many different pitches
whose rhythms are about the same, but not quite
on repetition; wheezes, rapid trills, catches
rippling over grass curved by the weight of dew
with its silver half-sheen in the half-light.

At midday above the crag a honey buzzard
mews to another as it circles
with hardly a movement of its wings.
Not a leaf stirs or tussock trembles
under its long breve, its fading call.

By evening emptied of all sound
a trick of shadow has made the valley a mouth,
a tongue of fire at the far end.
An almost pure flame, startling as a shout,
trails an incoherence of smoke from its forked tip.

45.

Pitch and tone, pitch and tone:
regarding intonation
none of the sages agree
on what we barely indicate
in stress and line break.

*The pitch of the voice*
*continually fluctuates*
*while we are speaking.*
Yes, yes, not what we mean,
but what we ought to mean.

We are perched in common speech
from which uncommon speech must climb:
thus a sheer physicality,
vocal cords more folds and contours
than interior harp.

46.

*I like that*, I do like that,
as though voice ascends from landscape
where we are composed in part
by, with and from others
whose rise and lapse we answer,

call to and answer,
a parliament of birds;
the carrion crow stiff-leggéd
as a distant relative
tentative at a funeral,

the savage robin on the gate
bleeping, “This is mine. This is mine,”
the nightingale, demure
poacher of other’s cadenzi
trilling round absolute pitch.

47.

It's time I put on a brave face
or was simply bare-faced
and stopped circling the truth
of the image of a mouth
for how a poem might just

begin to mumble on the page
even before the symbols
sharpen into focus
to much more than resources
of vowel and consonant,

a closed mouth being form
in repose, then parting
at an intake of breath, almost
as thought begins to be expressed
so I sense I know what just

48.

It *is* music rather
than sheer musicality
which brings on a monkish critical pitch?
Difficult, I suppose,
shifting from cloister to cloister

or their equivalences
while profanity beyond
ancient, well-dressed, snug-fitting
masonry hawks, gurgles or worse
from clyster to clyster.

In commerce and society
we do add to our daybooks
grace notes on the creation,
apologiaturi
on the Fall on Redemption.

49.

The sound of silence, beloved of bad poets:
what is it when it's at home,
someone waving and shouting behind a window,
the movement of the muscles round the lips
that the deaf read so exactly?

I doubt if there is such a thing as silence
for those of us with better hearing.
Even in outer space suited up
there is one's heartbeat and breathing,
tintinnabulation jingling in one's ears.

Silence is like life after death.
You'll never know it in this life.
Look, there is the life to come
its lips pressed everlastingly against the glass
mouthing breath and spittle.

## 50. *after Laforgue*

I’m only an idle man of moons
who makes circles in a pond
with no other plan in mind
than becoming pure legend
to those whose wishes were the sons

he could never quite engender.
Quite so. They were never born
and I can only just imagine
if I hide my hands, mandarin
fashion, in my sleeves and ponder

my own form in the mirror, a son
of sorts whose mouth I open,
whose breath I exhale without sound,
with a shape I simply can’t make as round
as Our Lady in the sky, the moon.

51.

I held the stone
the way I might clasp a lover's chin.
I regarded a crease in the stone,
a wry pursing of imaginary lips
along its whole composed length.

I spoke to the stone
drunkenly, but it didn't reply.
should I have then cast aside the dumb stone?
I wasn't listening , it may have replied
and I didn't catch what it said.

I'm sure I spoke to the stone
and its lips moved while I was relishing
what I'd said to it, the stone.
What was there to relish?
I missed the first words from a stone.

52.

M
O
U
T
H

S
P
E
A
K

T
R
U
T
H

53.

*Béons à la lune*
*La bouche en zéro*
—Jules Laforgue

0
0 0
0 0 0
0 0 0 0
0 0 0 0 0

0
0
0 0
0 0 0
0 0 0 0 0

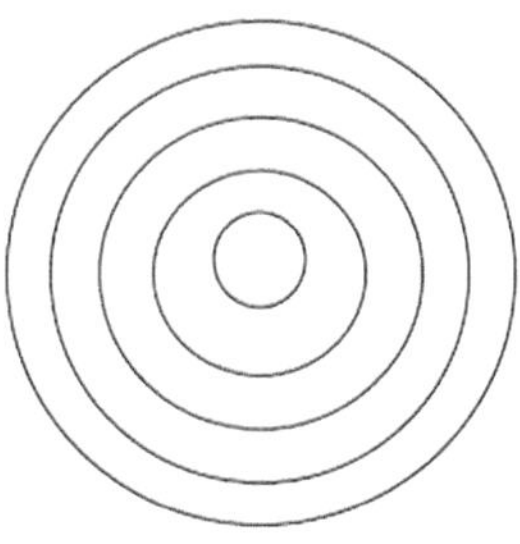

54.

The broken epic of a voice,
which never tells the same tale twice
and never knows if it damns or blesses,
which thinks it is Odysseus,
lips bitten and wrecked by ancient kisses,

interrupts the ill-tempered aria
rising to be transformed in an area
of sheer calm where it acquires
consonance, all the more eerie
by being pitched above the desires

of all of us below, whose outrageous
twists and turns of the tongue are easier
to distinguish, despite their grunts and hisses,
than love as love, whose sounding true requires
attention to what can soar away beyond us.

55.

Many
offer
up
their
happiness

Mouths
open
uttering
their
hate

Miles
off
ugly
toads
hop

56.

A toad sings in the garden
with a trill like a mobile phone
while the night begins to harden
as a mouth once sweet becomes
a zero someone turned to stone.

No change in the song of the toad,
which is simply calling for a mate,
no change in the eyes that glowed
except when a name is spoken
and a blank look comes alive with hate.

The toad's mouth doesn't open.
Its throat pulses each side of its head.
It has revived after rain has fallen.
In the hot summer under a rock
or rotting log it played dead.

57.

My strength of speech,
my force of utterance,
the power I had in words
was so dumbfounded,
was so gobsmacked

my voice moved
and emerged into the air
like a baby's dribble
after it has been burped
over its mother's shoulder.

So like a child
suddenly relieved
of wind inside its belly
I wailed and shed tears,
my voice too young or too old.

58.

Through your grace
grant us this grace.
Unveil your mouth to him
so he can discern
the second beauty you have kept hidden.

O splendour
of the light's eternal lustre,
who has ever paled so much
in the shadow of Parnassus
or drunk so deeply from its source

that he wouldn't seem nonplussed,
struggling to do justice
to what made heaven
a feeble parody;
your face all at once unveiled completely.

59.

Where are the mouthless presences?
Which is to say where are the opposites
to your colouring, your openings;
mouth, ears, eyes, their subtle tints,
and the unabashed pink and heat of your cunt?

Here might be your negative,
a Mexican wave of snow sliding
from the bluffs above the river
falling in slow motion leaving underneath
naked grey rock and scars of brown earth

as it hits the base of the bluffs
so a powdery mist bounces then ripples out
like a vast counterpane before stopping short
of Crested Buntings in a panic among the sedge
under pollarded willows at the river's edge.

60.

Her upper lip bee-stung;
a cold sore, did someone strike her
or a genuine gift of the tongue?
She fumbles a fresh till roll
which simply won't insert into the machine.

Copper high lights in her hair,
a henna rinse or the real thing?
Carmine nails at the ends of her long fingers;
is she Sophia who will give birth
to a serpent with a lion's head?

*I am sufficient for all who come.*
*I am speaking that can't be grasped.*
*I am the name of the voice and the voice of the name.*
*I am the sign of the letter*
*and the indication of division.*

61.

Botticelli's girl shows a hint of teeth,
a faint line below her upper lip, no more.
Her kisses might have threatened to draw blood
If liberties had been taken with her sense of self:
your lips just close round my upper lip in warning.

More than a hint of a baboon's incisors
emerge from Bacon's *Head I* and *Head II*.
No kisses, but one's face to be chewed off
even though no liberties would be taken
as a self rotates a snarl from wads of flesh.

In the *Study After Velázquez's Portrait of Innocent X*
a full set of teeth inside the pink lips.
No kiss of peace, but a high-pitched groan,
the self a Gregorian chant stuck on the one note
behind the yellow verticals of Nuremberg's lights.

62.

Remember the teeth:
my laptop not quite able
to download the full face of rival emperors
in Civilisation 4.
So only a pair dentures show

offering me
trade, defensive pacts, displeasure
at my alliances with more plausible bargainers.
I, too, might be a piecemeal head
on another's screen the goatee replaced

with designer stubble,
my thinning hair disclosing
a Presbyterian forebear's canny skull above a Celtic nose.
Not that I'm remotely capable
of pasting their shrewdness on to my soul.

63.

Of course, three hundred years back
a visage baring its teeth
in a painting signified madness.
So what are we to make of the average media star?
Why do they shake your hand and indicate, “I’m nuts!”

All those actors displaying dazzling teeth
like the glaciated Arctic horizon
seen from a budget flight across the Atlantic
while around them the flesh dries,
wrinkles, sags and has to be uplifted

by a faith in the life and fame to come
on this earth against a blue screen,
an Academy award for fifty years of survival
in the most trying conditions; harsh light, lousy scripts,
the mouth always withering into untruth.

64.

Despite the piece enduring an audience
just for thirteen minutes, twenty seconds,
the actress had to have her head braced
even though her training and experience
had given her the gift of absolute stillness.

It was so her moist crimson lips
could stretch, purse, pucker, wrinkle while babbling,
complaining, entreating, recalling, denying,
sometimes barely above a whisper
as though pleasuring something appalling.

*all the time the buzzing so-called in the ears*
*dull roar   scream again   her lips moving*
*all those contortions in the mouth   speechless*
*all her days   something she had to tell*
*god-forsaken hole   pick it up there*

65.

So here you have it from the horse's mouth,
direct, not by word of mouth.
Was he down in the mouth, shooting his mouth off!
Not to mention almost foaming at the mouth;
I almost had my heart in my mouth!

Mind you, he was all mouth and trousers,
never one to put his head in the lion's mouth
or his money where his mouth was,
always taking the good words out of her mouth
and putting them in some little tart's mouth.

You should have heard him mouthing off,
that she was born with a silver spoon in her mouth,
that butter wouldn't melt in her mouth.
Left a nasty taste in my mouth, I can tell you.
Fed up she said "Shut your mouth, arsehole!"

66.

Look at its mouth
when a voice gets religion,
how it stretches to the limit,
how it nails its lips to the Cross,
its tongue wagging like one of the thieves.

Look at that shape wavering round darkness
from thin, spit-flecked prohibitions.
primly they compress together
and promise paradise after years of delusion.
Parting they release bad breath, anger, nothingness.

*Thy tongue deviseth mischiefs;*
*like a sharp razor working deceitfully.*
*Thou lovest evil more than good;*
*and lying rather than to speak of righteousness. Selah.*
*Thou lovest all devouring words, O thou deceitful tongue.*

67.

Look at their mouths as they expound
a universal theory of everything.
Turn down the sound and just watch
the twists and turns of their lips
stress white, placid pink, hot air red

cyanose round a dark centre
where glimpses of teeth and a working tongue
might be discerned if you pay attention.
Turn the sound back up and you lose
even a sense of original language

as the lips contort beyond known limits
of vowel, consonant, click, burp and girn,
a white noise, a shrill pink squeaking,
cheeks flushed blood red, dark blue hiss
of air escaping a ruptured lung.

68.

A mouth within a mouth within a mouth,
a trinity of what might be said
and popping up quite unexpectedly
like jacks-in-boxes or the beast in Alien,
a trap sprung within a trap within a trap.

She said that you'd said that I'd said
and what opens as love closes its mouth
on the small bones of slights and grievances
their history and prehistory
as I think of an infinity of mouths

a mouth within a mouth within a mouth
containing voices louder and louder
finally sounding, if there were air to sound in,
at 10 to the power of 34 decibels,
the noise of the universe at the Big Bang.

69.

An over-riding speechlessness falls
upon those who receive the gift of grace.
They cannot tell what it is they've felt.
Cultivated speech is quite graceless,
the tongue prism-shaped splitting light.

To be over-ridden is my graceless fate,
my negotiations, my daily business
rendered otiose, artfully talked down
by diplomats whose gifts of insight
are on a daily basis, negotiable.

Thus Sophia from whom my care
was withdrawn, our great work
truthful and cost-effective,
stopped short by a diplomat of culture
his tongue split and no tuning fork.

70.

Maximum outcry uplifts the House.
Members open up their hearts.
Ministerial offences under the hammer.
Magicians of utterance try hocus-pocus,
magniloquent, obfuscating, unctuous, trivial, hypocritical.

Many others, unattended to, hear
mass, offering up their hearts,
mouthing often unplayed tuneful hymns.
Muted obscure, unrequired their hosannas
murmured outwards, upwards towards heaven.

Many of us temper honesty,
moderate our uncertainty towards hearts
mulling over unspoken terrible hurt,
make our understanding tentative, hapless,
moving others unobserved to hopelessness.

71.

Pitch and tone, pitch and tone,
an unheard of distinction
for the crew of the ship of state,
not the yacht, Britannia,
now dry-docked for conferences,

more fishing yawl losing its catch
from the pitch and toss, pitch and toss
brought by a gale of circumstance,
command blown away in the yowl
and yawp of wind in the rigging.

Not that the crew ever heed
their captain's voice, all of them orators
of the Six Words of Sincerity;
"I will repeat what I said,
I will repeat what I said."

72.

That tearing, tearing, tearing screech
which permitted little human speech
unless through a captain's megaphone
is now a mere simulacrum
in Mitja Močnik's home-made museum.

Two armies on each side of the Soca
scooped out caves like Al Qaeda
to live in, make sudden sallies from
into sheer noise not conversation,
into that screech punctuated by detonations.

Not a tree left standing, not oak or pine or beech.
In the museum punctured tops of tins
the Italians used to strain their pasta,
pieces of gas mask, a pink piece of denture,
that tearing, tearing, tearing screech.

73.

The mouth bellowing on the parade ground
has its own rhythm, its regularity
not to mention regulations.
From far away enough it almost harmonises
with the languorous shriek from a flock of crows.

The television mouth like the opening of a pitcher plant,
slightly sticky at the rim.
Press the remote and its recitative ceases.
I feel for the fly crawling across the screen,
but mercifully it flies off. What's that buzzing?

How I wish this argument against the argument
would simply shut up, but it keeps on
oozing noise like an imitation of honey,
this blandishment of language imitating language.
I should open my mouth and claim it's all about money.

74.

Our quicker-witted direct ancestors,
visionaries obsessed with hunting scenes
(Adjust the vertical hold Fred Flintstone)
could have listened and still exterminated,
refining stolen vowels to extend a repertoire

of lip farts, clicks and hisses though now every pixel
can tell a billion stories of life and death
as we in the present economic ice age
exterminate the vowels, the last signs of otherness
in each SMS we send with smileys below

narrow nostrils clarted with hedge funds:
call the accumulated snot capital
and a serious downturn in the markets,
the coming of the big white handkerchief,
courtesy, Ez, of Douglas, not Henry, Adams.

75.

A wonder sauntering ten feet above my head
away from the site of fire and smoke
in the narrow throat of the valley
black wings outstretched, in the stillness
twitching to maintain momentum,

scraggy head turning neither right nor left
legs trailing pedantically together,
a mosquito pterodactyl-sized,
the stork dragonish in its hunt
for the democratic frogs so common here

unaware of the dictator toad
whose neck pulses through the saggy folds
of skin and glands, an imitation of earth
silent, solitary, erroneous
beneath the rush of air down the valley.

76.

From the Gospels all else follows:
a first cause is so neat.
The Word is spoken presupposing a mouth
and all the shapings of our lips and tongue
round the movement of air follow from this.

But listen to that buzzing: insect wings,
legs rubbing, a stridulation
or the pylons humming, not a mouth open.
I prefer to take the words as they come
meaning almost anything or almost nothing

like the white noise from the radio
when it's tuned to a frequency
unoccupied by song or rhetoric or reportage,
the sound of the three degrees above absolute zero
we've been cooling towards for thirteen billion years.

77.

Can one truth last longer than another,
micro-measurements of vowel sound,
or truer when spoken in a preferred tongue
or tongue given preferment;
*"I do prefer / Polish to Czech"*?

Nobody'd prefer Deutsch over Yiddish,
would they? Neither language by itself
is more or less sacred than the other
except in the courts of prejudice
though I understand that living Yiddish withers

despite a literature,
despite musicianship,
despite good will begat by guilt.
Tongues do not last if there are no mouths
to give them housing, space for utterance.

78.

An efficient mouth lies in wait
lurking in the lies that make up
what priests and doctors might tell us.
We all achieve an efficient mouth
lipless, unhinged, jaw-droppingly so.

Shrinking towards efficiency
there's no cry, best keep the volume down,
from a mouth, no broken cry
unbroken in its persistence
through the night, unhinged in its way

howling beyond what anyone
might imagine could be human,
no cry once mouthed becoming mouthless
out there way beyond us, becoming
unbecoming, becoming itself.

79.

Gala concerts are the greatest draw.
Whole operas are too much to endure.
On the bandstand in the spa
a baritone and small orchestra
work through their repertoire.

Into parking places silver limousines sigh
and from the tumble children clutching flowers.
They would be angels so purely
are they dressed to honour Sunday,
but are not as they behave so poorly.

I watch them through the oratorio,
which is my life, which I fancy
has reached its extremity.
I'm an angel tugged to earth by gravity
now graceless, voiceless, without soul.

80.

I set down how I am Fearful.
Once in Gdansk I witnessed
a bag lady slapped by drunks.
"Stop!" I bellowed then slipped away
not waiting to be translated.

Viera and I prefer
seclusion. We've sat down
and in low tones beseeched
cowardice of one another
both fearful for the other's life.

Not so our daughter who pitched
into the skinheads at school
setting out to shame the shameless,
grades docked to C's for a term
their prank otherwise unpunished.

81.

*Swung by an arm … like flails;*
set down four thousand years after
*the children of princes*
*are dashed against palace walls;*
almost verse from scribe Ipuwer

reminding me of Tupperware,
ancient Egyptian vowels
being up for grabs. So let's rhyme
or half-rhyme, as you will,
by all means pitching at

a relish for atrocity:
here in this life on the grass
outside our flat a gypsy girl
was grabbed by skinheads, her arm snapped.
How does that grab you, grab me?

82.

Vowels vanish first, offals and bodily fluids;
blood, lymph, saliva, gleet and spunk,
leaving flesh to petrify,
The words shrivelled, lipless effigies
showing stained teeth, hands and feet crooked to claws.

The priests removed heart, brains, lungs and the rest
and placed them in canopic jars
only the consonants left
visible for poetry's
ceremony to revive an old doom,

words swathed in bandages, a mouthless groaning
rumoured to have supernatural powers.
You may rummage through pyramids
of dictionaries, unlock their secrets,
compile your very own Book of the Dead.

83.

I didn't find the mouth in Budapest,
that section of the museum being closed,
a smirking mouth, fiftyish, sixtyish,
in greys, reds, blues, ochres, a moist crease
under a moustache, a wrinkle in a rotten fruit.

So I went south to reality, his head tilted,
hands in his pockets, his mouth compressed,
amused, later claiming he was wondering
if he could borrow half-a-crown.
Got off at the wrong station before Trieste.

Did the boy from Philadelphia, broke in Venice,
ever truly smile? The last photographs
show a mouth pointed as a bee's mandibles
and sipping bitterness from the language.
Old men lose their sense of taste and smell.

84.

"*a narrow phosphoric stream*
*upon the waves of marble*
*that heave and fall*
*in a thousand colours along the floor.*"
And no pillar the same width as another.

Only Ruskin besotted enough
to go to all that trouble
measuring pillar after pillar,
irksome to Effie for whom the paradox
of stone and brick making San Marco

a perfection without exactness
she heard and saw only at a ball
where her bosom rose and fell,
her heart fit for a symmetry,
quickened by Austrian gallantry.

85.

In San Marco the colours shine
like the feathers on a linnet's throat
as we gaze from the shadow
gathered beneath the galleries
and round the great altar.

We tiptoe where we haven't been
and won't ever come again,
the queues being long and slow.
A faint noise of trumpets
and trombones for atmosphere,

though a theme of recognition
passes like a golden echo
from group to group, strangers
without fear, in good heart,
turned towards the steady sea light.

86.

What does an old drone do
after his brief act with Sophia?
Buzz off and hover beneath the eaves
of that old garden shed, English poetry
his wings dull as pewter, beard wistful?

One queen of the hive with bee-stung lips
is enough for any troubadour.
When she turfs you out of house and home
you can acquire a hooded, monkish look
to encourage misinterpretation.

The young queens have mated on the bee-loud isles.
A drone crawls on one of Ruskin's stones
that masons carved in the Gothic manner.
I coax the ageing insect on to a handkerchief
then flap him free to fly over the lagoons.

87.

Burnished glints in the furniture and glassware,
trumpet and trombone in Canzone e Sonate,
the hundred voices in my head unite
and answer one another, cori spezzati,
the dust motes dance in a light now blent.

I quit Gabrieli's sounding chamber
for my balcony and a cigarette
and the conversation of a thousand crickets.
they have no throats and rub their legs together,
a sound as soothing as the Cheshire cat's purr,

which is everywhere and nowhere and unseen.
Not all the world has to open its mouth to me.
Otherness sends to otherness. I can be seen
and heard as I rub my right calf slowly
with the heel of my left foot in sympathy.

88.

The bay isle almost completely built over,
a hermit's cell grown into a monastery;
to the right a second islet, flatter,
bristly with narrow scrubby conifers;
to the south a cloudscape that will bring warm rain

as across the water the monks' voices
drift with the breeze, a rise and fall of sound
in which neither vowel nor consonant can be discerned,
a line of sacred text, a melisma, a buzzing.
I could swim out there through the rain.

Half an hour of steady crawl
and I'd arrive almost naked, claiming that I had shed
all that was worldly down to my underpants.
Their sound carries to me, godly, wordless.
I imagine their prim lips twitching open.

89.

I could have lived on this mouthless island,
a windswept place of relative quiet
not to mention peace of mind,
the boom boom of the sea on the rocky side
bursting into caves at high tide.

What's that buzzing? Monks move among the bees
draped with fine nets over their faces.
They are figures from willow pattern porcelain
with their shallow triangular hats and thick gloves.
They lift a humming gospel from each hive.

With signs and gestures they move the bees
to their summer residence,
but one bends in slow motion
then turns to me with a golden beard
that seems to move of its own accord.

90.

Among the flowering apricot twigs
bees investigate a metallic sweetness,
scrambling from bloom to bloom
until the pouches on their legs swell
so they seem to trail saddle bags.

On the pot beside me a shiny bee crawls,
black abdomen, black thorax,
black mouthparts and antennae so precise
it could be a tiny motorcycle cop
dipping its head into blue speedwell.

What's that buzzing? More a rumble.
Thunder crawls around us all afternoon,
clouds forming mouth shapes about to speak
and make distinct the language of storm.
But no wind rises, no rain falls.

91.

Tiny bronze ants swarm across my hand.
They have rebuilt a yard from where
I boiled their nest to death last year.
They haul their white larvae to safety,
diligent beings that live in silence

with a composite black and white vision,
who communicate scent trails to one another,
no tones or vowels, perhaps vibrations
and a sense of sweetness from far off.
How much of our DNA could be similar?

We share processes, Krebs cycle
to produce formic acid and energy.
I should let them live, but my flowers must bloom
so bees can unzip their tongues into their nectar
and then dance at an angle to the sun.

92.

I have no general ideas,
only good will. I am even less aware
of the big picture. Stamp-sized is my vision
astigmatic with paramecia
flexing the luminous details of their outlines

an immeasurable close distance before my nose
for the intricacies of words,
the streaks on the tulip-coloured sentence
which others abjure for the phrase,
blocks on blocks on blocks of them.

Yes, I know that's really how we speak,
digressively, disconnectedly, brokenly,
but a poem is its own perfection of speech,
the sentence its redeemer, overwrought with stigmata,
which we fall short or, indeed, far too long of.

93.

Give me a long sinuous vista,
a fabulous dragon's tongue
neither Welsh nor Chinese,
of a sentence extended like a lawn
where I can stroll at ease

and listen not to idle chatter,
but to bird song, inhuman,
having nothing of my pitch or tone
though I might discern warning,
mating ritual, a claim to territory

and turn them to my own account;
omen, desire or mystery,
bird flight a sign on the sky's stave
seeming to write a music,
the measure of the measure of myself.

94.

Sophia has a hundred graphs
of intonation's rise and fall.
Her own voice is scrupulous,
likewise her husband's, instructing
champion ballroom dance teams

whose couples respond exactly
to tones of brass. I *would* pick on
music as my source of figure:
anything sounded requires
pitch and tone, pitch and tone

and an ear exact, exacting
as Beethoven's composing
late works, deaf to all save
memory, that unscrupulous,
unanswerable voice.

95.

Sophia's x-ray of mouths
for her doctoral thesis
on how we say what we say:
what were her mouths saying
showing their shadowy palate of tones?

A jaw bone taken from a Stone Age grave
is more definite than Sophia's pics,
delicately dusted down,
cleaned and exhibited.
What might it have said or sung?

It's flesh that makes conversation.
Let the little dancers at our lips and tongues
and there's not much left we can say.
The honey buzzard mews overhead.
The summer stream sniggers round its stones.

96.

I'll lie dead with my mouth shut,
not bound up with a grave cloth
with a top knot on my head
like an old-fashioned steam pudding.
Undertakers now have subtler arts.

I'll lie dead with my mouth shut.
Biographers can go whistle
for a life that is secret
and not worth investigation.
Write your books, write your books – I wish.

I'll lie dead with my mouth shut
though not I think forever.
What's that buzzing? Little dancers
limbering up in the ballroom
as my mouth falls open in a grin.

97.

Everything that has lived
from virus to Einstein is God.
Utter a simple word,
tree or stone, and we become
nothing less than prime movers.

Our garlic laden breath
will be affecting molecules
long after the dancers have performed
their last reverse and twirl,
collected their coats and departed,

long after the music stops,
long after syllables have ceased
to convey any meaning,
long after the sun suddenly bursts.
So creator, lift up your voice.

98.

## Musique Concrète

*for Edwin Morgan (1920-2010)*

Eleven strings do not an exotic instrument,
chromatic scale, the required dimensions
for a unified theory or complete universe make.
The radio initiates itself and sighs
            KWAAAAAAAGHGH SHKSHK

So we are at the very least distracted
leaving the key signature of what we will become
three degrees above absolute zero
or a very low probability
of going back upon ourselves and reincarnating

as moss or mouse, living fossil or even virus
therefore farewell aims and objectives
farewell grand design
crook a little finger or complex carbon bond
open your mouth and just be

99.

I saw him dismount and send his horse off
with a slap on its rump before he turned
and began to climb invisible stairs
hidden by Tien Shan's fog, his stick tapping
on marble he'd told me was the colour of stars.

Sophia floated above him her small mouth pursed
as though scolding or comforting a child.
"Your once flourishing breath is long departed.
You will never speak again on this earth.
Your last words buried you, broken-hearted."

She drifted down unpinning her hair
and walked beside him as he laboured up
his lips working hard for breath in the thin air.
Then he stopped, straightened and, as they vanished,
the old poet blazed briefly, a falling star.

## Sources and Notes

5. *from* THE SECRET BOOK OF JOHN – The Creation of Adam 15, 1 to 19, 10, *The Gnostic Gospels*, edited by Marvin Meyer, Harper 2007.

13. Recent DNA research suggests that a small portion of our genetic make-up may be Neanderthal although this more likely in individuals whose ancestry is Asian.

21. *from* THE SECRET BOOK OF JOHN – The Fall of Sophia 9, 25 to 10, 19. "She wanted to bring forth something like herself, without consent of the Spirit, who had not given approval, without her partner and without his consideration." *The Gnostic Gospels*, edited by Marvin Meyer, Harper 2007.

24. *from* 'Morgue' – Gottfried Benn, 1912
    Schöne jugend
    "Der Mund eines Mädchens, das langen im Schilf gelegen hatte, sah so angeknabbert aus."

28. *from* M.R. James – *The Stalls of Barchester Cathedral*

30. *from* 'Morgue' – Gottfried Benn, 1912
    Kleine Aster
    "Als ich von der Brust aus
    unter der Haut
    mit einem langen Messer"

34. Edward Lear's limerick:
    Who, or why, or which, or *what*,
    Is the Akond of SWAT?
    Is he tall or short, or dark or fair?
    Does he sit on a stool or a sofa or a chair, or SQUAT,
    The Akond of Swat?"

    See also the entertaining *Victoria's Little Wars* (Chapter: 'The Umbeyla Campaign') by Byron Farwell published in the Wordsworth Military Library editions in 1999.

37. Jean-Philippe Rameau: *Traité de l'harmonie réduite à ses principes naturels* (Paris, 1722).
A Jesuit mission to the court of the Chinese Emperor in the eighteenth century attempted to entertain him with what the regarded as the finest French music. The emperor apparently thought Rameau's music was barbarous. No doubt, his opinion of limericks would have been of the same order.

38. from 'Une Saison en Enfer' – Arthur Rimbaud
'Délires II Alchimie du verse'

J'aimais les peintures idiotes, dessus de portes, décors, toiles des saltimbanques, enseignes, enluminures populaires;
la littérature démodée, latin d'église, livres érotiques sans orthographe, romans de nos aïeules, contes de fées, petits livres de l'enfance, opéras vieux, refrains niais, rhythmes naïfs.

39. "dark red learning" (*hsüan hsüeh*) or profound learning was an aspect of neo-Taoism, which dominated Chinese philosophy from the third to the sixth century A.D. *hsüan* is used in Lao Tzu to describe the sublime mystery of the *tao*. It formed a major topic of "pure conversation" when scholars tried to arrest the decline of the tao.

40. *from* 'A Song of Wheel Tower in Farewell to General Feng of the Western Expedition' – Ts'en Shen (715-770), trans. Harold Witter Brynner (1881-1968)

41. *from* 'A Song of Running-Horse River in Farewell to General Feng of the Western Expedition' – Ts'en Shen (715-770) trans. Harold Witter Brynner (1881-1968)

42. *from* 'A Song of White Snow in Farewell to Field-clerk Wu Going Home' – Ts'en Shen (715-770) trans. Harold Witter Brynner (1881-1968)

43. *Tien Shan* a range of mountains of somewhat nebulous definition, but the northern limits border Kyrgyzstan.

45. Lines 6-8 I cannot recall where I read this, but read it I did – somewhere.

48. Line 14 a neologism from "apologia" and "appoggiatura."

50. *from* 'Locutions des Pierrots' XVI – Jules Laforgue (1860-1887)

Je ne suis qu'un viveur lunaire
Qui fait des ronds dans les bassins,
Et cela, sans autre dessein
Que devenir un légendaire.

Retroussant d'un air de défi
Mes manches de mandarin pâle,
J'arrondis ma bouche et – j'exhale
Des conseils doux de Crucifix.

Ah! oui, devenir légendaire,
Au seuil des siècles charlatans!
Mais où sont les Lunes d'antan?
Et que Dieu n'est il à refaire?

53. *from* 'Complainte de Lord Pierrot' – Jules Larforgue (1860-1887)
a rough translation of these lines might be
"Let's gape at the moon,
the mouth in zero"

57. is barely tangential to Dante's original

from *Purgatorio* Canto 31: lines 7 -21– Dante Alighieri

Era la mia virtù tanto confusa,
che la voce si mosse, e pria si spense
che da li organi suoi fosse dischiusa.

Poco sofferse; poi disse: "Che pense?
Rispondi a me; ché le memorie triste
in te non sono ancor da l'acqua offense."

Confusione e paura insieme miste
mi pinsero un tal "sì" fuor de la bocca,
al quale intender fuor mestier le viste.

Come balestro frange, quando scocca
da troppa tesa, la sua corda e l'arco,
e con men foga l'asta il segno tocca,

sì scoppia' io sottesso grave carco,
fuori sgorgando lagrime e sospiri,
e la voce allentò per lo suo varco.

58. A bit closer, but not a translation.

from *Purgatorio* Canto 31: lines 133-145 – Dante Alighieri

"Volgi, Beatrice, volgi li occhi santi,"
era la sua canzone, "al tuo fedele
che, per vederti, ha mossi passi tanti!

Per grazia fa noi grazia che disvele
a lui la bocca tua, sì che discerna
la seconda bellezza che tu cele."

O isplendor di viva luce etterna,
chi palido si fece sotto l'ombra
sì di Parnaso, o bevve in sua cisterna,

che non paresse aver la mente ingombra,
tentando a render te qual tu paresti
là dove armonizzando il ciel t'adombra,

quando ne l'aere aperto ti solvesti?

It is sometimes forgotten when Western newspapers and politicians work themselves into a lather over Muslim women wearing a veil when living in Europe that women in Christian Europe wore veils in the Middle Ages and even later in the Mediterranean countries

60. from *Thunder, Perfect Mind* in *The Gnostic Gospels of Jesus*, edited by Marvin Meyer, Harper 2005.

62. There's the gleam of perfect teeth in Sandro Botticelli's *Primavera* and I think in his *Mars and Venus*.

63. The computer game *Civilisation 4* by Sid Meier. I did get a more powerful computer so that more than teeth appeared.

64. The third verse is made up of phrases from *Not I* by Samuel Beckett. The actress, Billie Whitelaw, gave the first and definitive performance.

66. *from* Psalm 52 verses 2-4

69. Also 94 and 95. I am grateful to Dr. Renata Timková for the opportunity in 1998 to read her Doctoral thesis.

72. The Vojaški vojni muzej
The museum is located in the military camp of the Slovene army in Vipava. It was the first museum of its kind for the Slovene Armed Forces. The idea was conceived by its owner Sergeant Mitja Mocnik, who works in the military camp. The museum exhibits objects retrieved from the site of the battlefield and hinterland in the first firing-line on the Austro–Hungarian side in the hills around the river Soca. In front of the entrance to the museum there is a reconstruction of a firing-line.

74. Line 15 *from The Restaurant at the End of the Universe* by Douglas Adams.

77. Lines 14 /15 *from* Canzone 11, *The Orchards of Syon* by Geoffrey Hill.

81. Line 1 from *Canaan*, the title poem in the collection by Geoffrey Hill.

Lines 3-4 from a translation of the Ipuwer papyrus, which contains a poem called 'The Admonitions of Ipuwer'. A text which depicts an Egypt afflicted by natural disasters and in a state of chaos, where warfare, famine and death are everywhere.

I have forgotten where I saw a translation, except that it was over twenty years ago.

83. Verse 2 – There is a famous photograph of James Joyce as a young man. I recall reading that when asked what he was thinking about he replied to the effect that he was wondering if the photographer would lend him half-a-crown.

84. from *The Stones of Venice* – by John Ruskin, Folio Society edition ed. Jan Morris, 2001. Effie was the name of Ruskin's wife.

99. Lines 8-10 Qin Shih Huangdi, the first emperor of the Qin dynasty from 246-221 BC, unified the Chinese empire, built the Great Wall, standardized weights and measures, coinage, the width of wheel axles, and writing, created the terracotta army, burnt all the books except those relating to useful subjects such as agriculture, medicine, astrology, divination and the history of the Qin state and, finally, unsuccessfully sought immortality dying poisoned by the mercury in the elixir supposed to prolong his life.

He died while on tour of the eastern part of the empire but legend has it that he refused an opportunity to meet the Queen Mother of the West, the goddess, Xi Wangmu. A Tang poet nine centuries after his death wrote:

"His flourishing breath once gone, he will never speak again,
His white bones are buried deep, the evening mountains turn
dark blue."

www.ingramcontent.com/pod-product-compliance
Ingram Content Group UK Ltd.
Pitfield, Milton Keynes, MK11 3LW, UK
UKHW041845190726
13854UKWH00002B/731